THE STEP OF FAITH

By

Rev. William Andrews

The Step of Faith

Copyright © 2018 by William Andrews

All rights reserved. No part of this book may be reproduced or used in any manner without written permission of the copyright owner except for the use of quotations in a book review. For more information, address: revandrews@hotmail.com.

First paperback edition January 2019

Book cover by Seth Wright Kweku

ISBN 978-1-7342766-1-9 (paperback)
ISBN 978-1-7342766-0-2 (ebook)

Rev William Andrews

DEDICATION

This book is dedicated to my wife, Grace Andrews, my son William Kweku Andrews Jr, my daughter Grace Ewura-Esi Andrews, my daughter in law, Melissa Andrews and my grandchildren.

The Step of Faith

ACKNOWLEDGEMENT

To the many, faithfully praying and supporters of my ministry, especially Pat and Tracie McCaffrey, Mark Steck, Dickie and Ann Green, Mary Benson, Lynn Nell, Sherry Beard Ladd, Beth Quiaot, Pastor Fifii Orhin, and Pastor Granville A. Sr. I hold each of you in high esteem for being a blessing.

I also wish to acknowledge all of the prayer partners and supporters of my ministry; Seth Wright Kweku my associate in Ghana, and all of my family and friends for their support in a myriad of ways.

Rev William Andrews

PREFACE

This writing is about Faith, and it is buttressed by practicality. The motive behind the practicality associated with the book is inspired by the desire to give life to the book and make it relatable. The book covers the concept of Faith from the worldview and the Christian perspective. There are practical experiences dotted around the chapters of the book to accentuate points. There are also pointers from the bible which reflect the biblical angle of various points.

My more than 40 years of experience in ministry is brought to bear in this book with regards to Faith. Some of my Faith journeys have been highlighted in this book, showing my mistakes, lessons learnt and experiences gathered. This book couldn't cover every detail with regards to my knowledge in Faith; however, it serves as a platform to share some of my experiences with the world.

The underlining theme of this book is that Faith works. Having total faith in God works every time, but we need to bear in mind that there are precursors to this, and we need to know them in order to succeed; in the various steps of Faith we take in our lives, which is almost on a daily basis.

CONTENTS

DEDICATION III

ACKNOWLEDGEMENT IV

PREFACE V

CHAPTER ONE 1

DEFINITION OF FAITH 1

CHAPTER TWO: FAITH IN CHRISTIANITY 6

    THE DISTINCTION BETWEEN GENERAL FAITH AND FAITH IN CHRISTIANITY 6
    CHRISTIAN FAITH AT WORK 8
    FAITH IS CHRISTIANITY 11

CHAPTER THREE: TRIVIALIZING GOD'S DIRECTION IN TAKING A STEP OF FAITH 13

    MY FIRST STEP OF FAITH AS A CHRISTIAN 13
    IGNORING PRINCIPLES CAN COST YOU 22

CHAPTER FOUR: PRECURSORS TO TAKING A STEP OF FAITH 24

    THE WORD OF GOD AS A PRECURSOR TO TAKING STEPS OF FAITH ... 24
    PRAYER AS A PRECURSOR TO TAKING STEPS OF FAITH 27
    FASTING AS A PRECURSOR TO TAKING THE STEP OF FAITH ... 29

CHAPTER FIVE: THE PHYSICAL STAGE OF FAITH 30

    THE PHYSICAL ENVIRONMENT AND FAITH 30
    POSITIVE ENVIRONMENTS AND FAITH 32
    NEGATIVE ENVIRONMENTS AND FAITH 35
    EXCEPTIONS TO THE PHYSICAL RULE 37

    THE NEED TO CONSTANTLY FORTIFY OURSELVES 40

CHAPTER SIX: CHALLENGES AND FAITH............................ 43

    MY STEP OF FAITH TO ZIMBABWE 44

    THE NIGERIAN JOURNEY OF THE ZIMBABWEAN TRIP.......................... 50

    THE CAMEROONIAN JOURNEY OF THE ZIMBABWEAN TRIP 57

    THE ZAMBIAN JOURNEY OF THE ZIMBABWEAN TRIP 62

    MY ZIMBABWE EXPLOIT 64

    REFLECTION ON THE STEP OF FAITH TO ZIMBABWE............................. 73

CHAPTER SEVEN: NEVER UNDERESTIMATE THE BACKGROUND WORK OF GOD 81

CHAPTER EIGHT: FAITH CAN BE SHAKEN 90

CHAPTER NINE: CONCLUSION 101

Chapter One

DEFINITION OF FAITH

Faith is a complex concept that is sometimes difficult to evaluate because of its subjective nature. People have different definitions of Faith based on their personal experiences, their level of education, or social orientation. However, we can make an effort to bridge the gap in these differences of interpretation by relying on materials that can arguably be regarded as neutral or having the propensity of reflecting universal definitions, such as the Dictionary. The Macmillan Dictionary defines Faith as a strong belief in/or trust of someone or something, and a belief in a god or gods. The Oxford, Longman, and the Merriam-Webster Dictionaries all have similar definitions. In fact, evaluating the various synonyms associated with Faith, we would unearth words like; "Trust", "Belief", "Confidence" and "Reliance". The concept of Faith is grounded in the idea of totally surrendering to something else. It could be an idea, a concept, or a person.

The degree of submission or to what extent we can say one has totally surrendered to something else, is debatable, mainly because we can't measure it and we can't truly access it. In some instances, Faith is a concept that is difficult to explain. This is because Faith is a mental process that can't be easily weighed except by actions that evince one's belief in something. These actions themselves don't reflect "FAITH" they only reflect actions as a result of Faith, making the concept even more complex.

Faith being an abstract concept leaves us to settle on the actions of people in order to understand or evaluate their Faith in something. Through my voyage of life, I have realised that sometimes we can't draw conclusions about the level of Faith one has in anything unless we evaluate their actions. This means word of mouth is inadequate to speak for someone with regards to their Faith in something. In the same vein, one can only vouch for themselves with regards to the level of Faith they think they have and not for others. The interesting twist to this is that there are instances where we think we have Faith in something, or we think we have enough Faith till our actions speak otherwise.

I have witnessed a number of situations where people think they have Faith in something, but their actions later reveal they in fact did not. It is sometimes difficult to explain whether one's belief their Faith gave them a sense of pride, if they were genuinely convinced of their Faith, or they somehow lost Faith. My experience with such situations covers the physical and spiritual, where people claim or truly felt they had Faith in something or in God, but reflected the opposite. There have been times when people chastised others for not having Faith, or making others feel their predicaments were as a result of their lack of Faith or a "Faith" that isn't solid. This is usually characteristic within the Christian Faith.

I knew a pastor who was a strong advocate of Faith in God. He spoke, drank, ate, and slept Faith. Everything was centred on Faith. He constantly preached about Faith in God to everyone, which was a good thing. The problem was, when someone suffered a predicament, he blamed the person for lacking Faith in God. He told people they were broken because they had no Faith in God. When people got sick or had a dysfunctional marriage, he blamed it on their lack of Faith in God. His principle was that any negative thing in one's life was result of their lack of Faith in God. If Faith had a representative, he would have no doubt been the perfect candidate.

One day, this pastor was hit with a tragedy, the death of his son. It affected him so he was incapable of socially functioning. He couldn't find the strength to mount the pulpit to preach. His congregants were indeed alarmed, and demanded to know why he had lost his Faith in God, unable to persevere following the tragedy. They were compelled to ask as he had made Faith seem so simple, so simple it could not possibly be shaken. In theory, he was symbolic of what a devout believer encompassed. And now, from their perspective the epitome of Faith was unravelling. He was forced to accept the reality of the complexity of Faith. He told his congregants that he had realized Faith isn't a stroll in the park. Having Faith which should mean total surrender isn't an absolute concept that resonates with everyone the same way.

The complexity of Faith makes it necessary for us to be considerate with others with regards to their Faith journey. Having Faith, especially in Christendom is one that is characterised by varying experiences, good and bad. This in itself makes it necessary for constant self-evaluation, self-awareness, and preparation for various challenges.

Chapter Two

FAITH IN CHRISTIANITY

The Distinction Between General Faith and Faith In Christianity

The general concept of Faith and Faith in Christianity are not the same. In general, all humans have some form of Faith. It is innate within humans; it is almost instinctive in nature. This is reflected in our daily activities. In most instances, we are not aware Faith is the driving force behind some of our actions because they are mundane at best. Take for example, our belief that our legs will not fail us when we get up to walk. Or when we move our hands, speak, or any of the everyday acts we engage in, we believe what we envision will manifest exactly as we imagined. This is Faith. This is believing in something, and in this case, it is the belief in our ability.

Faith in Christianity

The concept of Faith in Christianity is more defined than the general definition or concept of Faith. The concept of Faith being an absolute belief in something also applies in Christianity. However, there is certainty with regards to who receives that absolute Trust, Hope, or Belief. In Christianity it is God. Faith in Christianity is the absolute dependence on God. God is the centre of Faith in Christianity. God in Christianity is the almighty that we can't see but we feel; we feel His works, and His wonders every day.

In Christianity, Faith is the evidence of things not seen. Faith says you have it, even before you do. Faith is Hope; hope that our Lord and Saviour, Jesus Christ will make our wishes come true. This is on the premise of Hebrews 11 vs 1, 6 (New King James Version (NKJV)) *"Now faith is the substance of things hoped for, the evidence of things not seen". But without faith it is impossible to please Him, for he who comes to God must believe that He is, and that He is a rewarder of those who diligently seek Him"*. This belief is usually associated with the hope that He would grant us our wishes, in most cases difficult wishes or what we would consider almost impossible or irrational. There are several stories that exemplify this. Some in the bible and others from my personal experience.

Christian Faith at Work

Several times I have placed my trust in God in difficult situations that people felt were impossible to escape from. I have also had instances where people doubted my chances to succeed in certain situations but I relied on God. One of the reasons for this is because my goals seemed irrational or out of the ordinary. Interestingly, God proved that He doesn't have to depend on human comprehension before He manifests.

I remember in 1983, myself and some other missionaries had a meeting in Port Harcourt, the capital and largest city of Rivers State, Nigeria. We were meeting to plan a crusade at a village behind the Port Harcourt zoo. This was supposed to be a precursor to planting a church in the community. That was my first time in Port Harcourt and my second time in Nigeria. I had been in Port Harcourt for two and one half months preaching at a local church. At the time, I still had very limited information on the area, but my wife had attended bible school in Bendel State, Benin City, Nigeria, and had made some pastor friends while there. When these friends and the congregants of the church I had been pastoring heard about what we were planning to do, they vehemently discouraged us mainly because a sea of preachers had tried several times to hold crusades there, but never succeeded. There were always light outages, and the back-up generators never worked. Clearly there were evil powers that constantly thwarted efforts to hold crusades there. At that point, there was no way humanly possible that a crusade could be held in that community.

When I heard of all the stories that threatened our mission, I didn't panic, neither was I discouraged. I instead declared that the crusade would happen by the glory of God, and there would be no hitches. The reason for my certainty was because I knew that if God sends anyone to do anything, there is nothing spiritually or humanly possible that could stop the person. I knew with God, all impossibilities were possible, and this manifested. We were able to have the crusade that lasted for 3 days. The electrical systems were perfect, with no need for the backup generator. At the crusade, not only were sorcerers delivered, but the sick were healed and souls were saved all to the glory of the Almighty God.

From the bible; Mark 5 vs 24-34, we can travel on a journey with a woman who has been bleeding for 12 years and even with the help of different doctors cannot heal, only worsen. It seemed impossible that she would ever get the healing she was desperate for. But she didn't lose Faith. She believed that she would be healed if she touched Jesus' garment (Mark 5 vs 28). It seemed silly that she believed that touching Jesus' garment would heal her when medical experts had tried and failed for years. It sounds and seems impossible, but her Faith made the impossible, possible. Her Faith led to her healing and Jesus said to her *"Daughter, your faith has made you well. Go in peace, and be healed of your affliction."* (Mark 5 vs 34 (NKJV)),

Faith is Christianity

From my story on how God came through for me and the story from the bible, it is evident that the difficulties or the impossibilities attached to what we are asking God for doesn't matter, what matters is our Faith in Him. This thought is reflected in Mark 11 vs 22-24 (NKJV) *"So Jesus answered and said to them, have faith in God. For assuredly, I say to you, whoever says to this mountain, 'Be removed and be cast into the sea,' and does not doubt in his heart, but believes that those things he says will be done, he will have whatever he says. Therefore, I say to you, whatever things you ask when you pray, believe that you receive them, and you will have them"*. Christ clearly highlighted the importance of Faith in our communication with God, which is through prayer. In order for us to get results, our prayers have to be grounded in Faith.

This is supported by Matthew 21 vs 22 (NKJV) *"and whatever things you ask in prayer, believing, you will receive."*

Faith in itself is Christianity. Christianity is accepting Jesus Christ as our personal Lord and Saviour. This can only be accomplished if we believe in Him. This means having Faith in Him, which is total surrender to Him. Hebrews 11 vs 6 (NKJV) perfectly reflects this *"But without faith it is impossible to please Him, for he who comes to God must believe that He is, and that He is a rewarder of those who diligently seek Him"*. Faith plays an important part in being saved and this is reflected in Ephesians 2 vs 8 (NKJV) *"For by grace you have been saved through faith, and that not of yourselves; it is the gift of God"*. If we don't have the belief that indeed Christ is our saviour, there is no way we can call ourselves Christians. This implies that anyone who calls himself or herself Christian and doesn't have Faith in Christ can't be a Christian.

Chapter Three

TRIVIALIZING GOD'S DIRECTION IN TAKING A STEP OF FAITH

I must admit that a lot of Christians take steps of Faith that are bound to fail. Taking a step of Faith as a Christian has to be guided by God's direction. Regardless of the level of Faith one possesses as a Christian, if you don't get God's direction, you are bound to fail. I learnt this lesson the hard way. As a Christian, my Faith was first tested in 1976. At the time, I was working as a textile worker, in Tema, a harbour city in the Greater Accra region of Ghana. I decided to quit my job as a textile worker, to chase a dream of living abroad.

My First Step of Faith as a Christian

My job was one that I had looked forward to and had struggled to get. Before I got the job, I had little support from my family. Although I wasn't from a poor family, I constantly had to struggle because I didn't have the support of my family. I was living with my grandparents, and when my grandfather died in 1973, my grandmother had to relocate to England to live with my uncle. At this point I decided to go see my grandmother's brother to ask for a job. He spoke to his friend about it, who was the personnel manager at Ghana Industry Holding Corporation (GIHOC). He in turn then spoke to his friend who was also a personnel manager at Ghana Textile Manufacturing Company (GTMC) to help me get a job there. During this time, those in positions that could influence job acquisition in particular industries made concerted efforts not to assist their relatives in securing employment as to avoid the appearance of nepotism. They instead spoke to friends in other industries to help their relatives get jobs in their organisations, and in turn, returned the favour by assisting the friend's relative in their own organisations. It was through this practice, I got a job as a textile worker at GTMC.

Trivializing God's Direction in Taking A Step of Faith

Working as a textile worker at that time was prestigious because they were paid well. During my time at GTMC, our benefits and salaries were only second to Tex Styles Ghana Limited (GTP). Getting the job was a turning point in my life. At the time, the factory was located at Tema, a harbour city in Ghana, so there was access to a lot of foreign things. With the salary and incentives I was receiving, I could comfortably provide for myself and friends, something I had not been able to do prior to securing the job.

After working as a textile worker for about 3 years, I gave a 2 weeks' notice of my decision to quit, and in September 1976 I officially quit my job. It wasn't a difficult decision because I had been considering the idea for at least 6 months. I was enthralled at the idea of leaving Ghana. Though I had not saved a lot of money, I felt I had to move. My destination then, was the Philippines. A different continent from mine, and about 13,277 Kilometres from Ghana, I had a pen-pal at the time who resided there, I was determined to go there. I knew I needed a plane ticket to get to the Philippines, and I couldn't afford it, but I had the Faith that I was going to get to my destination. My plan was to keep moving towards the direction of the Philippines, which was West from where I was.

Before I quit my job, I was living in one of the company's apartments, at Teshie, a suburb of Accra, and posh area at the time. After quitting my job, I had to move out of the apartment, so I left for my grandfather's house in Maamobi, a suburb of Accra, and a rough neighbourhood at the time. While at Maamobi, I met a young man who was about my age. He had been living in the area for years and had relatives in Abidjan, the major urban centre in Cote d'Ivoire, also known as the Ivory Coast. I didn't set out searching for someone that had relatives in Abidjan, but somehow, I met him, and from our conversations, it came up that he had relatives in Abidjan. I told him about my plans to move west towards Abidjan and he expressed his interest in helping me. He offered to host me when I arrived to Abidjan, but there was

Trivializing God's Direction in Taking A Step of Faith

one problem. He had no money, and no passport to go to Abidjan.

Since he didn't have travel documents, we couldn't travel on the same route. I was going to use the official route, through the border because I had a passport. He, on the other hand, had to use an unauthorised route to get into Abidjan because he wouldn't be allowed into the country since he wasn't an Ivorian citizen and he had no passport. So, I gave him some money to fund his trip to Abidjan, and I also gave him some items to sell upon arrival, so I could get some extra money when I arrived to Abidjan. Since he was supposed to host me in Abidjan, we decided that he take the lead and I would follow later. When he was leaving, he gave me the address of his relatives in Abidjan so I could them reach out to them when I arrived.

When I arrived to Abidjan, I located the address the young man had given me and I met him there. I experienced my first disappointment of the journey. He told me the items

The Step of Faith

I gave him to sell were seized by Customs officials. This meant the extra money I was counting on was gone. I knew he was lying about the items being seized. I came to the realisation that I was on my own in a country where I knew only one person. That person couldn't be trusted, amd I had very little money on me.

The young man's relatives were poor and I didn't want to be a burden to them, so I was there for about 3 days, and I hit the road again. I didn't know the country at all but I was still determined to move towards the West. With the funds I had, I left Abidjan for San Pedro, Ivory Coast. San Pedro was a harbour town and also a border town to Liberia. It was about 353 kilometres away from Abidjan. Since I didn't know anyone in San Pedro, my strategy was to look for any Ghanaian there and hope they would shelter me.

At San Pedro, I located the nearest Assemblies of God Bible School, but I wasn't welcomed, mainly because they didn't know me. After asking around, I was able to locate a

Ghanaian family who were Assemblies of God members. They were kind enough to offer me a place to reside. After some days in San Pedro, my money was almost depleted. As a result, I decided not to cross border into Liberia. At this point I had to think smart, and I made a decision to return to Ghana with the money I had remaining. Unfortunately, the money I had left couldn't take me to my base in Accra. It could only take me to Cape Coast, over 147 kilometres away from my home. The journey back home was a life changer for me. I almost lost my life on route to Ghana.

From San Pedro, I had a relatively smooth journey to Noe, the last Ivorian town closest to the Ghanaian border. I had nowhere to sleep the day I arrived, but I met a young man, about my age, whose mum was a sex worker and they gave me food and shelter for the night. The next day, I continued my journey to Half Assini also known as Awiane, a border town, and the capital of Jomoro Municipality, in the Western Region of Ghana. A man at Half Assini offered me a place to lodge for the night since I had no money to lodge in a hotel. He owned a laundry mat in town. This same man nearly sold me to be slaughtered.

At night, the man took me to a strange and isolated house by the beach saying he was going to visit some people. Upon arrival, there was no one in the house so he asked me to wait for him. I kept waiting, until at a certain point I felt something was wrong. I heard the Lord tell me to leave immediately, and I obeyed. I found my way back to the man's house. When he saw me, he was shocked and furious? He kept asking why I had left the place, and his actions showed disappointment. I still slept at his house that night, of course with one eye opened. In the morning, I confirmed my suspicion. Indeed, where he sent me that night was a place where people were used for rituals. That same morning, I received confirmation. I left his house and set off to Cape Coast.

Trivializing God's Direction in Taking A Step of Faith

Cape Coast is my hometown and about 220 kilometres from Half Assini. In Cape Coast, I stayed at my older half-brother's house. He was working at the school for the Deaf in Cape Coast at the time. I was with my half-brother for 2 weeks, then he gave me some money for my journey back home to Accra. I returned to my base in Accra, my grandparents' house at Maamobi. At this point in my life, I was lost.

I had quit my well-paying job, moved out of the nice apartment the company gave me, and had squandered all of my savings on an intended trip abroad, which failed. I was back to ground zero. Life from this point was a real struggle, but at this point, I hadn't realised my mistake. It was this situation which catapulted me to fulltime ministering, and it was only years later into my ministry that I came to realise my mistake. My mistake was that I had disregarded the importance of the precursors to taking steps of Faith. They are: Praying, Fasting, and Listening to God's voice before taking any step of Faith.

The Step of Faith

Ignoring principles can cost you

Trivializing God's direction before taking any step of Faith is perilous. In my case the ignorance of the importance of God's directions almost cost me my life on the journey I took; thankfully I was saved by God. I learnt a lesson, and every Christian needs to take this lesson seriously. Being a Christian doesn't negate the need to uphold the precursors to taking a step of Faith, the most important one being, hearing the voice of God.

Before I quit my job to embark on the failed journey to the Philippines, I was a born-again Christian. I had been born-again for about 18 months. I was a totally different person from who I used to be. I had lived a rough and carefree life. I smoked cigarettes and marijuana for fun and regularly drank high volumes of alcohol. I also used to visit witch doctors and sorceresses for all sorts of help. I was lost until I visited a Pentecostal church. Whilst at the church service, I started shivering in my seat as I listened to the preacher share

Trivializing God's Direction in Taking A Step of Faith

the word of God. This wasn't the first time I was listening to the word of God, but it was different that day. I felt the power of God so much so that I had to believe in God. At that point, the yoke of bondage was broken in my life. It was a yoke of oppression that restrained me from coming to Christ. After that day, I was never the same, as I continuously yearned for more of God. But even with this change in my life's trajectory, there was still the need to observe important factors before taking the step of Faith. Being born-again didn't make me immune to the principles needed in taking steps of Faith. Getting God's direction is the ultimate requirement in taking any step of Faith, and this can be achieved through the combination of hearing His Word, Praying, and Fasting.

Chapter Four

PRECURSORS TO TAKING A STEP OF FAITH

From my experience, I can say with certainty that there are key precursors to taking steps of Faith and growing Faith. Over the years I have learnt that these precursors are Hearing the Word of God, Praying, and Fasting. These are components that can't be compromised when we either want to exercise or build our Faith.

The Word of God as a Precursor to taking steps of Faith

Just as the kind of food we eat affects our growth and strength, the kind of words we ingest influences our Faith. This implies that for us to grow our Faith, there are specific things we need to feed our minds with, and this is the Word of God. Romans 10 vs. 17 indicates that Faith comes from hearing, and the message is the word of God. It isn't just reading the word of God but taking Him at His word. It means doing what God says, this can only happen if we believe His Word. When I became a Christian, I had one guiding principle; believing in God's Word. I always tell myself that I have no choice as a Christian but to believe in the word of God; I better believe the report of the Lord. God's reports are His promises, fundamental among them being that He will always provide our needs (Ephesians 3 vs. 20; Hebrews 11 vs. 6; Philippians 4 vs 19; Proverbs 10 vs 3; Psalm 34 vs 10; Psalm 81 vs 10). Believing in His word, which must be consumed regularly gives the assurance of what to expect when we have faith in Him. His words never fail. Regardless of what happens, we succeed in whatever we set out to do if we have Faith in Him.

One important thing that Christians need to be aware of is that reading the bible is different from reading a secular book or novel. The word of God is powerful and sharper than any two-edged sword, which can pierce the heart, joints, and marrow (Hebrews 4 vs 12). The word of God must not be joked with or taken for granted. We shouldn't read the bible as a storybook; we need to meditate on it when we read. The bible needs to be pondered on. Let's say you find yourself reading John 3 vs 16 (NKJV) *"For God so loved the world that He gave His only begotten Son…"* This statement could be read and no cords would be struck, mainly because it was taken literally. The statement has to be broken down and pondered upon. *"For God so loved the world"*, we should reflect and conclude that we are part of the world, and if God loves the world, then it means He loves us. This doesn't end the process; we need to go further and ponder on why God loves us to the extent that He sent His Son to die for us. It must be because He wants to save us from something and prevent us from perishing. This pondering process should lead us to meditation. It is a simple fact that for us to understand the word of God, we need to go through this process.

When I was a nonbeliever, I never understood the word of God. I had listened to several preaching messages, and read the bible, but I never understood the word of God. This was because I never meditated or pondered on the word. We can't ignore the importance of meditating on the word of God, and this is evinced in the book of Joshua 1 vs 8 (NKJV) *"This Book of the Law shall not depart from your mouth, but you shall meditate on it day and night, that you may observe to do according to all that is written in it. For then you will make your way prosperous, and then you will have good success"*

Prayer as a Precursor to Taking Steps of Faith

Prayer also goes concurrently with hearing or reading the word of God. It is an important factor in the field of Faith. The bible in 1 Thessalonians 5 vs 17 asks us to pray without ceasing. This requires us to constantly pray at all times. Prayer is the breath of a Christian, which signifies the lifeline of any Christian. It is one of the major things we need to survive as Christians. Just as breathing is paramount to our survival as human beings, as Christians we can't afford to stop praying if we want to survive spiritually. If we aren't breathing properly, it means we are sick. The same applies to praying; when we aren't praying properly as Christians it means we are sick.

Prayer isn't just a means for us to make requests to God, it is also a means of properly communicating with God, which goes beyond just making requests. It is a way of being in God's presence. Sometimes we don't necessarily have to say anything during prayer, but God can still access our hearts since we are in His presence. This implies that even in silence we can still communicate with God. Romans 8 vs 26-27 (NKJV) holds true to this; *"Likewise the Spirit also helps in our weaknesses. For we do not know what we should pray for as we ought, but the Spirit Himself makes intercession for us with groanings which cannot be uttered. Now He who searches the hearts knows what the mind of the Spirit is, because He makes intercession for the saints according to the will of God"*.

When we believe in something or someone, we need to constantly be in touch; this reinforces our stands that we believe in them. The ultimate question is how do we claim to believe in someone when we are not properly communicating with the person? This further highlights the importance of prayer, with regards to our belief in God on any level as a Christian, including our Faith in God.

Fasting as a Precursor to Taking the Step of Faith

Fasting is also an important component of Faith in Christendom. Fasting usually goes with prayer as it too has been evinced several times in the bible, in scriptures like; Acts 13 vs 3 and Luke 2 vs 37. Fasting is a way of humbling ourselves as reflected in Psalms 35 vs 13. Fasting is also a way of clearing any obstacle that is standing between God and us. When we want to take any step of Faith, it is paramount that all blockages between God and us are cleared, and fasting ensures that we achieve this.

Chapter Five

THE PHYSICAL STAGE OF FAITH

Listening to the Word of God, Praying, and Fasting all gives Faith a spiritual face. But we can't ignore the physical when it comes to Faith. The physical influences the level of Faith, or the endurance level we need when we want to exercise our Faith. The nature of the environment can influence the effort we need to put in to exercise our Faith. The environments we find ourselves in, with regards to the circumstances, situations, or settings, can either make it easy or difficult for us to exercise our Faith.

The Physical Environment and Faith

To some extent, I feel that when we talk about Faith or compare the Faith of people, there is a need to evaluate different components, key among them being the physical environment. There are instances where people don't understand what it means to have Faith. They don't see the need to have Faith, because life is more about survival to them. This line of thought can be bolstered by people's experiences from different countries. Imagine asking children in the middle of the war in Syria, what they want to be in the future. What do you expect them to say? They have seen gunfights and bombings for years. They might not even know what Faith means.

What if we go to the jungles of the Amazon and ask them about having Faith? They would likely know nothing about Faith. All they know is living in the jungle and trying to survive. Even in poor neighbourhoods in our cities where people eat from the dump, poverty has affected most of them to the extent they can't think right. With low self-esteem, they can't exercise Faith. I have seen families use cardboard boxes as shelter in counties in Southern Africa during the winter. I have seen them walk with no shoes in this same weather. How do you ask people in such situations to have Faith? You can't compare these people with those who find themselves in an ideal environment.

Positive Environments and Faith

A psychological imprint that things are possible is usually created when we find ourselves in productive environments. This mindset makes it easier to have Faith in things or situations, such as believing that God will grant a request. In this sense, the positivity of the environment or events gives some level of motivation to believe in things. This implies that exercising Faith becomes easier compared to a chaotic environment, or in a system that frustrates us.

When I first went to the United States (US) from Ghana in 1989, I discovered a totally different world. In the US, few people pray saying, *"Lord give us this day our daily bread."* This is because most fridges are almost always full of food. You can take a loan for a house, a car, a trip, and so many other things that can make life comfortable, as long as you have good credit and a good income that qualifies you for the loan. There are scholarships that can be applied toward a litany of opportunities. In the US, if you really need a job and want to work, you will get a job. It may not be what you desire, but it will pay some bills. But such conditions as this are luxuries in many other parts of the world, especially in most African countries. This causes most people in these countries to worry about a lot of things, unlike those who might find themselves in well-developed and stable countries such as the US. This constant worrying tests their Faith almost on a daily basis.

My experience in different countries revealed this important fact to me. It was and still is easier for me to exercise my Faith in the US, than most other countries I have been to over the years, especially African countries. For example, if I had started my ministry in the US the support would have been overwhelming, as compared to where I started it in Ghana. In the 70's, America's support for global evangelism was high, while it was quite low in Ghana. Also, there were other avenues to make money in the US which wasn't available in Ghana at the time. If I had started my ministry in the US and didn't get any support, I could have worked part-time to pay my college bills, and there was also the possibility of securing assistance from a mission organization in helping me to raise funds. This wasn't the case in Ghana. It was quite difficult, so I had to intensify my Faith so I would not give up.

When I was in school in the US the ex-servicemen had their tuition paid for by the government. This was new to me because there was nothing like that where I had lived prior to moving there. I wonder how many countries have such benefits. I have always said that a disabled person may not bother to be healed in the US because of the benefits from the government. Some disabled people in the US receive discounted housing, free education, free health care, food stamps, etc. This is uncharacteristic in many other countries. Due to welfare, some people don't bother to work. It is almost as if there is no need for Faith, because it is a given you will be provided for. But as Christians, having Faith in all situations is a necessity. Having Faith in itself is Christianity, which is having Faith in God at all times.

Negative Environments and Faith

When we are in an environment with a lot of problems to deal with, it sometimes becomes difficult to believe in things, because the physical circumstances cause you to doubt whether things will indeed work out. A system where it is difficult to access proper food, get access to transportation, or gainful employment. Even a lack of good education can lead to a lot of frustration and kill the need to believe or have Faith. This has led many to give up on God. Imagine the state of mind of those who live in swamps in some West African countries. I have seen people struggle through mental illness due to hardship. How do you tell a slave that you can live like the master or mistress? Some of these people see no light at the end of the tunnel. In a situation like this, for us to survive, and continue to believe in God, we have to make an effort to be strong and not give up. This implies that, in the midst of certain obstacles, or difficult situations, mainly with regards to the physicality of events, the intensity of our Faith needs to be heightened.

However, we need to be sensitive to the hardship that people go through and not assume that when we ask them to intensify their Faith, they will immediately respond or be uplifted. There are some instances where they might have already intensified their Faith, but become hopeless because they see no improvement. The fact remains that in such cases, it takes the supernatural power of God to change their mindset. This is possible as it is written in Matthew 19 vs 26 (NKJV) *"With God all things are possible."* It is also possible for God to change any situation as it is in 1 Samuel 2 vs 8 (NKJV) *"He raises the poor from the dust and lifts the needy from the ash heap."*

Young people have said to me, "*Rev Andrews, I want to die.*" They say this because they see no need to live in an environment where there is so much hardship and no sign of hope. I have seen people, especially preachers chastise people for not having Faith. I feel it is wrong. You can't ignore the physical environment when it comes to Faith. When I am faced with situations where people have lost hope and don't see the need to have Faith in God, I understand them and try to encourage them instead of chastising them. I often use my own life story as an example. A story that is filled with loss, disappointment, and hopelessness, but later changed for the better. I tell them how Faith in God can change our situations for the better, and it has been effective in encouraging them in most cases.

Exceptions to the Physical Rule

It is a fact that there are physical dimensions to the level of Faith required in some situations. *"easier in working systems",* difficult *in systems that don't work"*. However, there are exceptions to this. Regardless of a conducive environment having the propensity to motivate us to easily have Faith in God, there can be another outcome, at least for some people I have met. I have met people whose reason for not believing in

The Step of Faith

God is because they find themselves in a system that works. Good roads, easy access to food and transportation, and their argument was that the system makes things possible and not God. To them, there is no need for God. In cases such as this, it is not uncommon to have people believe in systems or those in the system rather than God. The US has some of the best physicians in the world, who can treat a number of conditions. This fact gives some people the impression that there is no need to pray to God since those with the power to cure are here on earth. The essence of having Faith or hope becomes blurred in this instance, making discipline a key component to maintain Faith in God.

Disregarding God over systems or people in systems is wrong because regardless of what people think, God is the creator of all things good, so there is no way He can be taken out of the equation of our lives. There is always the need to have Faith in Him.

The Physical Stage of Faith

We also need to bear in mind that even though finding ourselves in conducive environments can influence our level of Faith positively; it also has the tendency to make us complacent. Through my journey of life, I have had first-hand experience in how the comfort of some environment decreased the intensity of my Faith. For example, when I started my ministry in Ghana in 1977, I used to constantly pray for sumptuous meals. It was a luxury to me. I had to constantly have Faith that I would get such meals. When I relocated to the US, the Faith in having these meals diminished, mainly because I didn't have to struggle to get those meals since it was affordable and easily accessible. At a certain point, the things I was depending on God for drastically diminished, and the prayers (communication with God) also diminished. In as much as life was better, it wasn't a good sign because complacency started to settle in, and I reduced my communication with God.

The Step of Faith

The Need to Constantly Fortify Ourselves

As Christians we need to always fortify ourselves, especially reinforcing our belief in God, regardless of the environment we find ourselves in. Neglecting this practice can be dangerous to our Christian lives and our Faith in God. There have been instances where I have met people who easily had Faith that God would answer their prayers in a conducive environment, turn around and lose Faith and give up, immediately finding themselves in a difficult situation. I have taken my time to study this trend over the years, and I have discovered that it is mainly because prior to the difficult situation, things were easy and smooth, so there was no need to intensify their Faith in God; but intensifying our Faith in God is needed and a requirement for every Christian, because the devil is always skimming and on the lookout to steal from us (John 10 vs 10; 1 Peter 5 vs 8). This is one of the reasons why Christ fortified Himself with fasting and prayer (Matthew 4 vs 2-11). Christ could have relaxed and not bother about anything; after all He is Christ, but He saw the need to prepare for the difficult times.

On the other hand, in as much as it doesn't seem advantageous to exercise Faith in an environment that doesn't work or is problematic, it can also be of advantage to some extent. When one is able to pull through in difficult circumstances, it eliminates the complacent behaviour some of us exhibit when we are having a smooth ride. Obviously, this doesn't happen to everyone, but it needs to serve as a way of seeing the positive in a negative situation. This implies that as Christians we should see the difficult circumstances as motivation to build and fortify our Faith in God.

The physical environment can't be ignored. To do so, sets a dangerous path to failure for ourselves with regards to our Faith in God. In any situation or system we find ourselves, good or bad, the tendency to lose Faith in God remains. It might have different degrees, but it is present and this makes it even more important to fortify ourselves so as to be steadfast in the Lord. From my experience, for this to happen, we need to be disciplined at all times by constantly communicating with God, and abiding by His word. Also, encouraging ourselves with inspiring materials such as books is also essential. Over the years, there have been books that have helped me keep my Faith in the Lord. Personally, I have read Christian books such as; 'Tortured for Christ' by Richard Wurmbrand, 'Men Who Heard from Heaven' by Gordon Lindsay and many other great books, that have inspired me to always keep my Faith in God.

Chapter Six

CHALLENGES AND FAITH

From previous chapters, it can be deduced that my journey through life hasn't been smooth, especially with regards to exercising my Faith. One thing I have learnt throughout the years is that our Faith in God will always be challenged. Sometimes even the environment we find ourselves can challenge our Faith in God, as explained in earlier chapters. Most times, questions like *"What if I fail?"* may come up, but failure shouldn't be in the vocabulary of a believer. Even when we have the fear of failure, it shouldn't deter us from having Faith in the Lord. The Lord says we shouldn't be afraid (Jeremiah 1 vs 8). So, we need to know even in the face of challenges that He is in control.

The Step of Faith

My Step of Faith to Zimbabwe

My step of Faith journey to Zimbabwe, in 1980 didn't make sense to a lot of people, and there were a lot of challenges. I foresaw some of them before I started the journey, but I had to be strong and believe in the Lord. I had no savings for the journey, not even money for a plane ticket, and I didn't know the people in the country I was travelling to, but when God spoke to me to go, I had to.

I was in my room one afternoon, in Ghana, and God spoke to me through a dream and asked that I go to Zimbabwe, then it was known as Southern Rhodesia. This was a place that was over 7,558 kilometres away from me, however I didn't know this for certain at the time, but I knew it was quite a distance from me, and I had to go through a number of countries to get there. At that time, I didn't know what my mission there was going to be. It took me 6 months to finally embark on the journey. I had to make plans for the journey. During this period, I read the word of God, prayed, and fasted about the journey, an important exercise that can't be taken for granted in taking the step of Faith. On this journey, I was faced with countless obstacles, most of which I didn't anticipate, but since I asked for God's direction before I took the step of Faith, He always saw me through.

At the time, my ministry was going well in Ghana. I was heading an Assemblies of God church in Madina, Ghana. It was a pioneer church, and the only Assemblies of God church in that area at the time. It was thriving and one of the fastest growing churches I had ever been a part of. It had a wide range of congregants from all walks of life. Typically, this was the time for me to relax and watch the church wax on. But I was told by God to move.

It took me 3 months after I got God's direction to inform the church about my decision to leave. I gave the church a 3 months' notice of my intention to leave. At this point, a lot of people didn't understand my motive for wanting to leave a church I was a pioneer pastor in, at such a critical stage. For the next 3 months the members and elders of the church tried to persuade me to stay. They thought the motive for my leaving was material, so they kept asking if they could do anything to motivate me to stay. They asked if they could change my furniture or increase my salary, thinking if they improved my living conditions I would stay. I understood them and sympathized with them. I made them aware that on the surface it would be better for me to stay with them, but since God had directed me, I had to obey. Even after my explanation, some of them still didn't understand, but they assisted me and I appreciated it.

The church took an offering for me to support my journey. It was nowhere close to half of what I needed for the journey, but at least they made an effort. I remember one of the members, a bank manager at the time, Mr Nyarko bought me a plane ticket to Nigeria. I told congregation I was going to Nigeria because I didn't want to appear crazy from their perception. It was obvious I didn't have the kind of funds needed to make a trip to Zimbabwe which was much farther than Nigeria. The church paid me my salary so they knew my financial status and there was no way I could have had the needed funds to travel to Zimbabwe. I also didn't want to be discouraged any more than I had already been. In actuality, the trip to Zimbabwe was supposed to take me through Nigeria, Cameroon, Zambia and finally to Zimbabwe.

Before I left Ghana, I made an effort to find someone that could introduce me to anyone that resided in Zimbabwe, considering the fact that I knew no one there. I asked a friend, Stephen Appenteng, who is now a pastor, to take me to Archbishop Duncan Williams, the founder of Action Chapel International, a well-known pastor by then. I didn't know Archbishop Duncan Williams personally, but Stephen Appenteng was friends with him. The aim was to ask if he had any member from Zimbabwe, since he had an international congregation, and his church was close to an international hostel which was just around the Airport in Ghana. When I went with Stephen Appenteng to see Archbishop Duncan Williams, the reception was warm. After the exchange of pleasantries, my friend introduced me, and I told Archbishop Duncan Williams about my intention to go on a missionary trip to Zimbabwe. I asked if he had any members from Zimbabwe who could host me and he indicated that he didn't. Just when I was about to leave, a young boy walked in, he was from Zimbabwe and a student in Ghana who was residing at the international hostel. Immediately he walked in, Archbishop Duncan Williams hugged him, welcomed him, and after exchanging some pleasantries, Archbishop Duncan Williams suddenly turned to me and said *"oh this guy is from Zimbabwe!"*

I told the boy that I was going to Zimbabwe and I knew no one there so I wanted the address of anyone there who could host me. He was willing to help, so he gave me the name and address of his church, Zimbabwe Assemblies of God Africa (ZAOGA). I thanked him and Archbishop Duncan Williams, and I took my leave with Stephen

Appenteng. However, before I took my leave, Archbishop Duncan Williams offered to help me get someone that could host me in Nigeria. He indicated that his cousin lived in Lagos, Nigeria and would be willing to host me. From our conversation, it was suggested that he would have to talk to his cousin about it since he was in Ghana at the time. I returned a few days later for a response.

When I returned, Archbishop Duncan Williams shared with me the good news that his cousin had agreed to host me. He gave me his name and address in Lagos. He even took me to go see his cousin's mother, who resided in Ghana at the time. At this point, everything was going smoothly. I had someone to host me in Nigeria, and an address of a church in Zimbabwe that I presumed would be willing to host me. The only setback, it seemed at that time, was the money needed for the trip from Lagos, Nigeria to Zimbabwe. Even though this was a cause for concern, I wasted no time in sending the church in Zimbabwe a letter and my photograph, informing them that I was coming.

The interesting thing is that I didn't ask for their permission, or their views on whether they would be willing to host me. I also left no return address, so there was no way they could have contacted me even if they had wanted to. I did this because God had spoken to me to go on the journey and I was standing on that. I was all fired up to go, disregarding every formality. Looking back now, I think I should have given a return address and waited for their reply, since there's always the human aspect that should be considered; we shouldn't inconvenience others in our quest.

The Nigerian Journey of the Zimbabwean Trip

I started my journey about a month after I sent the letter to the church in Zimbabwe informing them of my visit. With the plane ticket Mr Nyarko got for me, I was able to take a direct flight from Accra, Ghana to Lagos, Nigeria. I had already communicated my arrival date and time through Archbishop

Duncan Williams, to his cousin who resided in Lagos, when he accepted to host me for some days at his residence. I was sure that he was going to come for me at the airport.

I had a relatively smooth flight to Lagos. Upon arrival, I patiently waited for Archbishop Duncan Williams' cousin to pick me up at the airport. At that time there were no mobile phones, so contacting him at that point was virtually impossible. The only option available to me at the time was to wait and hope he would show up. Minutes turned into hours, then I came to the realisation that I was on my own. So many thoughts flooded my mind as to the reason for the disappointment. I never got any answers to the many questions for the disappointment.

Lagos being a place I had never been before, had me at a loss. I didn't know what to do at the time. I prayed for God's guidance and asked Him to lead me. It was late at night and I didn't have enough money to book a hotel. I slept at the airport that night and planned to search for Archbishop

The Step of Faith

Duncan Williams' cousin, if he didn't show up the following morning, since I had his address from the Archbishop.

In the morning, he had not shown up. I headed out of the airport, halted a taxi, and asked to be taken to the address I had. I arrived to the address, which was located in a posh area and discovered he didn't live there. I was disappointed but I had to keep moving. I asked the taxi driver to take me to any Assemblies of God church, and he took me to one at Ojuelegba, a suburb of Surulere.

When I arrived to the church I met the head pastor who was on his way out. I approached him and introduced myself. I also showed him my credentials as an Assemblies of God pastor. I politely asked him for a place to lodge for some days before I continued my journey. It was obvious he was in a bad mood. The only response I got from him was "*I'm going out!*" He said this in a very harsh tone, brushing what I said aside, and immediately walked out on me. After the pastor walked out, the caretaker of the church approached me and apologised to me. He had witnessed what had transpired and wasn't happy about it. He left his post, took me to his house, a very small building, where he stayed with his parents; they fed me, and allowed me to rest.

After about an hour at the caretaker's home, we found our way back to the church. After about 3 hours, the head pastor came back and apologised for his rude behaviour earlier. He then explained to me that he couldn't host me in his house, which was near to the church, because he didn't have enough rooms. It was just two rooms for him and his family. He suggested that I sleep at the church just like others who didn't have anywhere to lodge. From that time, the reception was warm. They fed me and treated me well until my departure. I was there for about a week. During this period, I preached twice at the church, Good Friday and Easter Sunday. After the preaching, an offering was collected for me, as was the norm at the time. Although it wasn't a lot, it helped on my next voyage.

The Step of Faith

My next stop was Bendel State, Benin City, Nigeria. All throughout my journey, I didn't know any of the places I had been or was going to, I only relied on my geographical knowledge to keep moving towards Zimbabwe from any of the states or countries I found myself. Bendel State was one step closer to my final destination, and coincidentally it was where my fiancé at the time, now my wife, was attending bible school. I had communicated with her via letter weeks before leaving Ghana about my intention to embark on a journey to Zimbabwe. I never told her about my route, except that I would be going through Nigeria. So, at that point she had no idea I was going to pass through Bendel.

I took a bus from Lagos State to Bendel State, it was an over 314 kilometres journey. When I arrived, I halted a taxi and headed to my fiancé's bible school. I had the address before I got to Lagos. I got to the school and located her. She was shocked and happy to see me. I ended up lodging at the boys' dormitory of the school. After staying in Bendel state for some days, I decided to use the little funds I had left to head to Aba, Nigeria, which was about 236 kilometres away. I remember having a conversation with my fiancé then, and I told her I didn't have enough money for the journey, and she thought I was joking, because it was a crazy idea to embark on such a journey with limited funds. It wasn't only until years later that she came to know that I was serious then.

Since I didn't know anyone in Aba at the time, my strategy was to find an Assemblies of God church when I arrived. Upon my arrival to Aba, I halted a taxi and asked the driver to take me to an Assemblies of God church. He ended up taking me to one at 224 Clifford Road. Apparently, it was one of the biggest Assemblies of God churches and also popular in the area at the time. At the church, I met the assistant pastor in his house, which was on the same compound. I spoke to him about needing a place to lodge for some days before I continued my journey. He indicated that I could sleep at the church. While we were still talking a man

The Step of Faith

came to visit him. The man, Mr Morris Okodiri, was a merchant, and somehow, he was roped into our conversation.

Mr Morris was interested in my trip and was willing to help. He had just arrived from a business trip in Germany. He indicated that he would have bought my plane ticket to Zimbabwe but his goods hadn't arrived, so he didn't have enough goods to sell for cash. At this point we continued talking, and I mentioned a 14 day Cameroonian visa I had acquired in Lagos. I told him I had Faith I was going to go to Cameroon even though I had been cash-strapped throughout the trip. Immediately, Mr Morris told me that he knew a businessman, Mr John Ndukwe, also known as Long John, of blessed memory, in Doula, the largest city and the commercial and economic capital of Cameroon. Being a merchant, Mr Morris travelled a lot and Cameroon was one of the countries he frequented, where he met Mr John at a church where he worshipped when he was in Cameroon, Eglise Pentecôte

(Pentecostal Church). He only had the church's address and not Mr John's, so he gave me the church's address.

For the 3 days I was in Aba, Mr Morris was very helpful. He showed me around Aba and made me feel at home. He also took me to where I purchased a plane ticket to Doula, Cameroon. For me to go to Cameroon, I had to board my plane from the airport in Calabar, Nigeria. So, I left Aba for Calabar by bus, a 109-kilometre journey.

The Cameroonian Journey of the Zimbabwean Trip

I arrived to Calabar in the evening. I employed my usual mode of operation. I halted a taxi and looked for an Assemblies of God church. I spent one night at the church and headed to the airport in the morning. I left for Doula, Cameroon, which was about 475 kilometres away. At the airport in Doula, Cameroon, there was a misunderstanding with the duration of my Cameroonian visa and the time allocated for me to stay in Cameroon. Ultimately, I was detained. I was confused and lost the entire time because I didn't understand what the

The Step of Faith

Immigration officers were saying. They were speaking French, a language I don't understand a word of. At that point I could tell from their gestures that they were going to deport me. A Nigerian Pastor who had taken my pen earlier to fill out his immigration form saw me being detained and came to my aid. We struck up a conversation when he borrowed my pen earlier. It was through that conversation I realised he was a Pastor. He became my interpreter since he understood and spoke French fluently.

From the interpretation, the immigration officers were asking me how long had I planned to stay in Cameroun. Through my interpreter, I responded that I had been given a two-week Cameroonian visa from Lagos, Nigeria, which was in my passport as 14 days. But when I arrived to the airport in Doula, Cameroon, the inspecting immigration officer who I had first met before being detained, wrote in my passport I would be staying in Cameroon for 15 days, instead of 14-- the allocated duration of the visa. The whole basis of the misunderstanding was the discrepancy in the allocated duration of the visa and the duration of my stay the immigration officer had written in my passport.

During the interrogation, the immigration officer that wrote 15 days instead of 14 days was nowhere on sight to admit his mistake. It was almost as if the entire saga had been staged to facilitate my deportation or possible extortion. I kept telling them it wasn't my fault, that it was a mistake by the immigration officer, but they wouldn't budge, insisting it was a criminal case. Eventually, the senior immigration officer released me with the help of my interpreter.

When I released, I found my way to Eglise Pentecote. It was a very small church, I met the caretaker of the church, and I asked for Mr. John Ndukwe's residence. The caretaker didn't know where it was, but he told me Mr. John's son was at a nearby school attending classes. I located the school, met a teacher there, and told him I was looking for Mr. John

Ndukwe's son so he could take me to his father. He was called and the teacher asked that he take me home.

When he took me home, I met his mother and I was told Mr John had dashed out. He had just returned from a two-week business trip from the US, through Nigeria. I waited hours until he returned. When I saw him I immediately recognised him. I had seen him at the Calabar airport earlier. Apparently, we boarded the same flight to Douala, Cameroon. I couldn't have missed him because I noticed he was quite popular at the Calabar airport. Immediately, I indicated that we were on the same flight, and he corroborated it. The next words that came out of my mouth were; *"God has sent me to Zimbabwe and I have come for you to buy me my plane ticke*t". Without any hesitation, he said *"God sent you!"*

Mr. John and his family were very accommodating. The night I first met him, he offerred take me to a hotel, all expenses on him. I respectfully declined. I had to apply wisdom. I was asking him for a plane ticket to Zimbabwe,

Challenges And Faith

which was quite expensive at the time, and even though he didn't know me, he was still willing to pay for my stay at a hotel. I couldn't have been insensitive as to demand for more. I suggested that I stay at his house, but he insisted on taking me to a hotel saying his children would disturb my peace. I told him I didn't mind. I finally convinced him to give up on the idea of me lodging at a hotel. He then took me to another house of his, where he lodges the boys who worked for him. It was a huge house, and nothing short of luxury.

I stayed at Mr. John's for approximately one/ week. I was well taken care of. I lacked for nothing. For two Sundays I was also given the privilege of preaching at Englise Pentecote, where Mr. John worshipped. Mr. John kept his promise and purchased me a one-way plane ticket to Zimbabwe. The flight was a transit flight from Lusaka, the capital city of Zambia, so I had to apply for a Zambian visa from their embassy in Cameroon. Unbeknownst to me before I arrived to the embassy, having a round-trip plane ticket was one of the requirements to obtaining a Zambian visa. This was going to be a problem since I only had a one-way plane ticket. But through God's divine intervention, the officer who issued me the visa ignored this requirement.

With my Zambian visa secured, I prepared to leave Cameroon. Mr. John gave me a lot of things for my Lusaka journey. I was gifted with a lot of clothes, food items, and forty dollars, even though it was on short notice. I held one last service in Mr. John's house with his family, and they were delighted about it. I gave my thanks, said my farewells and headed to Lusaka, Zambia, not knowing anyone in the country.

The Zambian Journey of the Zimbabwean Trip

I arrived to Lusaka, Zambia from Douala, by air with the transit ticket Mr. John had bought for me. It was a long flight, about 4,661 kilometres. At the airport, I was detained for no reason. I was held for almost an hour. Somehow the immigration officer didn't notice my transit visa. After I kept pushing to know why I was detained, the officer apologised and allowed me to go. Almost immediately a customs officer stopped me, and asked to where I was going. When I responded I was a preacher, I was asked to show my bible, which I did. This is what gained me entry into the country.

My flight to Zimbabwe was a few days away, I needed to be in Zambia for some days. I needed a place to lodge, and I needed to be frugal with the money I had remaining. I had twenty pounds sterling and forty US dollars on me, so I resorted to my mode of operation. I halted a taxi and asked to be taken to the nearest Assemblies of God church. The taxi driver took me to a Canadian Assemblies of God missionary.

I approached the head pastor of the Assemblies of God church, who was a Canadian missionary. I introduced myself as a missionary from Assemblies of God Ghana, and was heading to Zimbabwe. I told him I needed a place I could lodge for some days. He was cold and bluntly told me that we were not the same. He said the Assemblies of God church in Ghana was for the Americans and the ones in Zambia were for the Canadians. He told me I was supposed to have enough money to book a hotel, that he couldn't help me. Then he told me they had a member who is Ghanaian, Mrs. Dzokoto, of blessed memory, who was a professor at the school of nursing in the area. The nursing School was a well-known school, and since the taxi driver knew it, he asked the taxi driver to take me there instead.

I located Mrs. Dzokoto and told her I was heading to Zimbabwe, and needed somewhere to lodge for some days before my flight to my final destination. She was kind enough to give me shelter and fed me throughout my stay in Lusaka. When I was leaving for the airport to fly to Zimbabwe, she was kind enough to pay my taxi fare.

My Zimbabwe Exploit

I arrived at the airport in Harare, Zimbabwe, the same day I left Lusaka, Zambia. It was a 495-kilometre journey. The trip was relatively smooth, but the atmosphere in Harare was tense. I arrived exactly two weeks following Zimbabwe's independence. I was detained and questioned just as I had been at the airport in Lusaka. They wanted to deport me because I didn't have a round trip plane ticket. I had to give the immigration officer the address of the church I was there to visit. The officer placed a call to the church from the airport. He got the administrator on the phone, and told him about my arrival. The administrator confirmed that I was in the country to visit them, and advised that he would be picking me up from the airport.

I waited over 4 hours for the administrator to arrive. He was accompanied by the Sectional Presbyter of Harare District. The immigration officer asked them to provide a return ticket for me before I could be released. They were able to persuade him to release me by explaining that they were a big church and purchasing a return ticket for me wouldn't be a problem. Quite convinced by their comments, the officer ordered my release.

The Step of Faith

From the airport, my host drove me to the residence of the denominational leader, Reverend Ezekiel Guti. He welcomed me and gave me a room at his bungalow to lodge. All through my stay at his residence, which was about 2 weeks before he travelled out of the country, we ate together, and I was given presidential treatment.

I wasted no time in starting my ministerial work in Zimbabwe, as plans were already set for me since they were expecting me. I held the first evangelical service at a local Zimbabwe Assemblies of God Africa (ZAOGA) Church in Kumbuzuma, a suburb of Harare. It was a five-day service and the church was filled to capacity with people who had come from different suburbs, hungry for the Word of God. It was an amazing service as souls were saved and all manner of diseases were healed. The service spoke to me, as I became sure of my mission in Zimbabwe. God was using me to touch lives, spread His word, and heal people.

The service in Kumbuzuma was a springboard that launched my preaching across Zimbabwe. After the service in Kumbuzuma, I held another service at a ZOAGA Church in Tafara, also a suburb of Harare. It too was a five-day service. The service was highly publicized as a result of the first service in Kumbuzuma. It was also filled to capacity. There were also miracles and healing, and multitudes gave their lives to Christ. I remember how in one of the services, a boy with a crooked arm got his arm straightened just by my touch in the name of Jesus. During the entire five-day service, there was always no room for people when there was an altar call for people to give their lives to Christ. All of this happened during harsh weather conditions, during the cold winter season.

All of the services I held in Zimbabwe were during the cold winter season, mainly in rooms with no heating systems. But the rooms were always filled to capacity. There were instances where people who had heard me preach in their suburbs followed me to other suburbs so they could hear the

The Step of Faith

word of God again. The territorial evangelist of ZAOGA also constantly accompanied me to the different towns and suburbs where I held services, and his support was enormous.

I remember moving from Tafara to Bulawayo, the second-largest city in Zimbabwe, after Harare, it was about 455 kilometres apart. We had to drive for over 5 hours to get to our destination. I accompanied Reverend Ezekiel Guti, and I was asked to preach to ministers and church members who had come from the whole region for a ministers' council meeting. I was supposed to preach for one night. However, because of the mighty power of God that evening, the people demanded that I preach again the next day at a special Sunday afternoon service called the Big Sunday, where thousands of people from various churches were present. That service was wonderful. I was elated as thousands were touched by God. Many were healed and delivered. However, there was one thing I wasn't pleased with, was how the crowd rushed to touch me at one point. They were using me as a point of contact for a touch from God in areas of expectations in their lives; but I felt worshipped, which didn't sit well with me.

Immediately after the service in Bulawayo, I moved over 296 kilometres away to minister in two cities: Gatooma, now known as Kadoma and Hartley, now known as Chegutu in the Mashonaland West province. Then I proceeded to Chiredzi, a small town in the Masvingo province in southeast Zimbabwe. It was about 450 kilometres from Gatooma (Kadoma), and we drove for over 6 hours to get to the final destination. I also held services at Fort Victoria, now known as Masvingo, also in the same province as Chiredzi, about 196 kilometres away, and an over 2-hour drive journey. Then I proceeded to Norton, also known as Chivero, a town in the west of Mashonaland province. It was a 316 kilometre journey, and the drive took over 4 hours. All the services held in these cities were wonderful. God used me to do great things in His name at every service.

The Step of Faith

During my entire stay in Zimbabwe, I was never hurt even in the face of much danger. This was a miracle. Zimbabwe being a newly formed country, still had a lot of people with unresolved enmity. There were a lot of danger zones. Some people were still guerrilla fighters even after independence. A lot of towns were usually filled with booby traps and land mines. It wasn't easy travelling around at that time, but God saw us through and kept us safe throughout, even when we walked through areas prone to land mines. This was a big miracle to me and the other ministers who usually accompanied me.

I was in Zimbabwe for 3 months, and generally, my exploits in Zimbabwe were good. God used me to heal and deliver a lot of people, and I was able to lead many more to the Lord. While in Zimbabwe, many people I came across bestowed me with several favours. I was also blessed with many opportunities. I remember having a business proposal from Mr. John, the man who purchased my ticket to

Zimbabwe, to set up a business and claim a 10% stake in it. I also remember having the opportunity to lead a group called the Fox with my friend in Zimbabwe. We were going to receive support from the parent group in South Africa, where all of our needs were to be provided for and we were to be paid handsomely. I never pursued any of these opportunities because I felt and knew I had a greater purpose in Zimbabwe, which was to do God's work.

There were also negative experiences during my exploit in Zimbabwe. The man who was the territorial evangelist of ZOAGA, the second in command to the denominational leader, Reverend Ezekiel Guti, was used by God to help me. He was quite older than me; I was a very young man. The territorial evangelist of ZOAGA was a good man and a well-respected man of God. He was helpful when I had to move around Zimbabwe. He took me around. He saw how God was using me to touch people's lives at my young age and became jealous. This is something that is not uncommon in

Christendom, since being Christian doesn't stop us from being human and being prone to human shortcomings.

After some time preaching across Zimbabwe, the jealousy of the territorial evangelist of ZOAGA caused him to constantly boycott my invitations from other churches. At the time this was happening, the denominational leader, Reverend Ezekiel Guti had travelled out of the country and I was staying in the territorial evangelist's house because I needed him to take me around the country for my missionary work. When I noticed the jealousy, I didn't tell anyone about it, I just moved on.

Although the territorial evangelist was boycotting my evangelical work, he was still a man of God. I felt he had only given into jealousy. The jealousy of the territorial evangelist was a problem and it didn't make sense for me to cause more problems by making noise about it. I had touched a lot of lives for God in the few months I had been in Zimbabwe, and I felt I had fulfilled the assignment God had given to me. At this point, I requested to go back to Ghana, and the church purchased me a plane ticket to return home.

Reflection on the Step of Faith to Zimbabwe

My entire journey from start to finish was one of total dependence on God. I became a different man as Faith moved me from one point to the next, even with the little money I had on me. There were challenges but God always came through for me. Before the journey, I knew it was going to be challenging because there were obvious obstacles. I had limited funds, I was discouraged by people, I didn't know anyone in the places I was going to and I didn't know the places. All of this made my mission seem impossible. Looking at the journey at every point, we can easily tell that it was filled with challenges but God always made a way.

We should know that when we are taking any step of Faith, we can be faced with challenges from people we don't know or systems we know or may not know of. I was detained at every airport except Lagos, Nigeria. The reasons for this were either because I lacked some requirements needed for my travel or because of some misunderstanding. There were times I was up to date with all requirements but somehow, I was still detained. This goes to show that there are times when things may feel or look on course, but we might still face challenges or blockages. For me, when I was detained, I was released by some divine intervention, because I totally depended on God.

I constantly struggled to get accommodation when I was moving around, because I couldn't afford the cost of a hotel. This was an obvious challenge from the onset of the journey. It was a reality that couldn't be taken lightly. This type of challenge comes up frequently in our lives as humans. This is a challenge that has to do with the obvious. There is usually no surprise element in this case. This sort of challenge manifests when you need to achieve something or get something done, but you obviously don't have the means to make it happen. The truth is, we can't always get everything in place to facilitate all of the life journeys we seek to embark on.

Challenges And Faith

It is just human reality there is almost always the limitation of resources. What we need to do in this case is to always rely on God to provide. The bible says God will always provide our needs (Matthew 6 vs 25-34; Philippians 4 vs 19). When I was faced with this sort of challenge, in the form of not having places to lodge, I relied on God, and I ended up getting places to lodge and I was fed by complete strangers.

However, we shouldn't stop using wisdom even when we solely rely on God. The bible says wisdom is key (Proverbs 4 vs 6, 8 vs 11, 16 vs 16). We would perish if we lack wisdom (Hosea 4 vs 6; Isaiah 5 vs 3; Proverbs 10 vs 21). Wisdom is something we all need as humans. It will be out of place to say to ourselves that since we rely on God we should just go with the flow. There should be wisdom guiding our steps. I had to go to Zimbabwe, and I didn't know anyone there. I was certain God had ordained the journey, but that didn't mean I shouldn't prepare for the journey before I set off. I made an effort to get people who could host me in Zimbabwe even before I left.

The Step of Faith

Even though it was difficult to get connected to people in the 80s, as a result of communication limitations, I still made an effort. There were no mobile phones or social media platforms, but I resorted to the best way I knew, talking to people face to face. This helped me get an address in Zimbabwe before I set off.

I also moved with a strategy that worked for me. When I found myself in a place I didn't know and needed help, I took the initiative of looking for churches. Even though not all the churches received me warmly, the majority of them did, and it helped make my journey a little less rough. Another strategy I employed throughout my journey was proper human relations. I was always particular about how I spoke to people and treated them, and this resulted in positive outcomes for me. Looking back, if I wasn't able to properly engage Mr. Morris, who connected me to Mr. John who in turn bought my plane ticket to Zimbabwe, I probably would have struggled more to get to my final destination. If I wasn't accommodating to the preacher I met on the plane to Zambia, I probably would have been deported. Because it was only when he stepped in to interpret what the immigration officers were saying, that I was able to convince them to let me go, when I was detained.

Having a strategy doesn't mean we should always rely on an already existing one, or someone else's. This is because life journeys are different and a strategy that worked for one person might not work for another. This is where the dependence on God arises again. We need to always pray for guidance and wisdom from God; He alone can give us that winning strategy (Ephesians 1 vs 16-17; James 1 vs 5; 1 King 4 vs 29).

Finally, on any journey we find ourselves, we need to know that dealing with people's thoughts is something we are likely to encounter. There is the possibility that people we know can pose challenges to us, even those who should be helpful to us or those who should be spiritually mature. This is usually as a result of their perception on what we intend to do, or are doing. We need the wisdom of God and the sole reliance on Him to overcome all of this. When I decided to embark on my journey to Zimbabwe by leaving the church I was pastoring in Ghana, both the elders and the church members tried for months to persuade me to abandon the journey. I understood them, because they didn't get the message directly from God as I did, and I didn't expect them to understand. I had to make sure I managed the situation. Already their effort to stop me from going was enormous, and it wouldn't have been wise to intensify it by telling them I was embarking on a journey that was virtually impossible to go on. So instead of saying I was going to Zimbabwe, I told them I was going to Nigeria, and the pressure was reduced.

During my evangelism in Zimbabwe, out of jealousy, the territorial evangelist of ZOAGA was boycotting my missionary work at a point. This was a man of God and he saw what God was using me to do in people's lives. He ignored the work of God and how my evangelism was promoting it. This is a man who should have known better that God's work comes first and not our personal needs or envy, but the devil had his way. This should tell us that there are instances where people that we wouldn't expect to pose any challenge to us, end up undermining our efforts. When I was faced with this challenge, I had to apply wisdom. I decided to leave, because staying could have caused some animosity and perhaps an even bigger problem that might destroy the work of God we had done so far.

Ultimately, I learnt a lot from the journey to Zimbabwe. Important among them was to solely rely on God regardless of the situation. When we take any step of Faith, we need to condition our minds that we might be faced with challenges. It is usually not a smooth ride, even when the step of Faith is ordained by God. We need to know that the devil will always test us and wants us to fail. The devil even tested the master, Jesus Christ (Matthew 4 vs 1-11). Once we have it in our mind that these challenges that come about during our

The Step of Faith

steps of Faith are just distractions from our main goal, we can always have that assurance that nothing can stop us from reaching our final destination. We might not see it, but once God has ordained our step of Faith, He will always be working behind the scenes to make sure we succeed.

Chapter Seven

NEVER UNDERESTIMATE THE BACKGROUND WORK OF GOD

What we need to know is that God is always working (John 5 vs 17). From my experience in my Zimbabwean journey, I got confirmation that God is always working behind the scene. There were solutions to challenges I faced and these solutions were as a result of the occurrence of parallel events I had no control of and didn't anticipate. But they converged to solve my problems. Sometimes because we can't see how things end, we tend to underestimate God's work. As humans, it is understandable that we get frustrated over certain happenings in our lives but do we really ask ourselves if those happenings are all geared towards saving us?

Let's say we have to get to work and our car won't start, then later we are told the bridge we travel across to go to work

The Step of Faith

has collapsed, resulting in the deaths. Probably this might not be the narrative, maybe the bridge never collapsed, but what if our being on the road would have led to a fatal accident. Another thing that infuriates most of us is waiting. The lack of patience in God and even in the physical is something most of us struggle with. Let's say we get angry because the waitress/waiter didn't serve us on time, while we were waiting for about an hour, then something happens; all of the people who were served got food poisoning. Or probably the delay was some sort of divine intervention designed to save us from getting on the road when we would have wanted to, saving us from an impending accident, or mugging. There are usually some "what if" questions we sometimes fail to ask ourselves.

I have met people, both young and old who got frustrated about not getting married when they planned, or not having kids when they wanted. There have been bad times and people end up losing Faith in God because of this. The question we don't always ask ourselves is, what if God was saving us from an impending disaster? What if getting married at our ideal time results in frustration in our marriage, what if the people we love become a thorn in our flesh, what if the child we want badly, turns out to be a burden and not a blessing after some years? We wouldn't be able to know this or give a definite answer, because as humans we can't always see how things end from the beginning. We don't know everything, only God knows everything (1 John 3 vs 20; Proverbs 15 vs 3; Isaiah 55 vs 8-9; Psalm 139 vs 1-6; 147 vs 5).

Because we sometimes don't know, we don't appreciate God's work, and the things He saves us from, so we end up not having Faith in Him, as much as we should. It is fair to say this is part of human nature to some extent and it is embedded in us, but there is always a need for discipline and for us to remind ourselves of the need to have total Faith in God. He is always working on our behalf, and with Him, there is no challenge we can't face.

The Step of Faith

I have had situations where things have happened to me and I didn't understand why God allowed them to happen, until years later. I remember how I used to wonder why I had to go through the discomfort of a disease even before I was born-again till I gave my life to Christ. It used to be frustrating, but many years later I got to realise that, the so-called disease might have actually saved me.

God had been using me for years to heal people, both adults and children, but I also badly needed to be healed. I needed healing from a disease in both legs for almost a decade. I had sought doctors, herbalist; even witch doctors for help before I gave my life to Christ, but all to no avail. For years I had said to the Lord, *"How can I take the message of deliverance to nations whilst I am diseased in both feet?"* Many times, I heard the devil mock me that I can't be healed. As a result of the disease, I couldn't show my legs and I had to always wear trousers. I went to the bathroom in trousers, swam in trousers, and partook in sports in trousers. I remember how I used to wake up at dawn or wait until late at night in bible school before I took my bath.

The dormitory in the bible school had four people in each room, with two communal bathrooms. Just like those of a typical secondary school in Ghana, privacy was a luxury. However, I was able to hide my disease. No one knew my problem except one of my friends who I confided in. He tried to help, by taking me to a place where they tried using herbs to heal me, but it didn't work. The disease tormented me for years, which was liken unto Goliath torturing the Israelites.

I prayed for years and nothing happened. There were times I would close my eyes, pray, and hoped that when I opened my eyes, I would be healed, but nothing happened. It was frustrating. At one point, I didn't understand how God could use me to heal people, and I still wasn't healed. But the word of God says my strength is made perfect in weakness (2 Corinthians 12 vs 7-10.), which clearly implies that you being

The Step of Faith

sick doesn't mean God can't use you as an instrument to heal the sick. God clearly had His plans for me, and knew best.

One day in 1978, I suddenly had a strong feeling that it was time for my healing. I had been diseased in both legs for 9 years at the time. The Lord spoke to me and asked to take a razor blade and shave the hair on my legs. I obeyed the Lord according to His word. The shaving was painless, it felt like having a beard shaved. The next day the rashes on my legs had disappeared. As my legs were getting hairy in weeks, the rashes came back. God told me to shave my legs every 3 days. I did so and in 6 weeks God told me to stop shaving. God healed me completely.

This was a disease that didn't only limit me from physical activities and frustrate me, but also humbled me. It somehow regulated my life. I never got comfortable with the disease, so it always humbled me. Knowing the kind of person I am, a strong-headed individual, one that was fond of engaging in perilous activities for fun, I knew without the disease I would have gone to the extreme. The limitation the disease placed on me even restricted me from engaging in sexual relationships before I became born-again. Also, the disease drew me to church before I gave my life to Christ. The disease was a blessing in disguise. It helped me to stay humble and not to be arrogant since I was being used by God to heal others. Of course, when I wasn't healed, I didn't see things this way. I kept pushing to be healed and kept asking God why I had to go through the discomfort of having the disease. Now, I can proudly say it all worked out well for me, because it put me in check and made me mature. Looking back now, I should have been patient and allowed God to heal me in His own time, because He makes all things beautiful in His own time (Ecclesiastes 3 vs 11).

I had a friend who went to be with the Lord. He said, Faith has a sibling and the sibling is called Patience. If we truly have Faith, we will have the patience to wait. The question is *"what are we to do during that waiting period?"* What we need to do

The Step of Faith

is to keep on believing. Doubt may set in, but remember you can walk on water by standing on the word of God. Peter stood on the word of God when the Lord said, "*Come.*" When our Faith starts to waver, we need to focus on Christ (Matthew 14 vs 22-33).

What distinguishes Christians from others is the ability to stand on the word of Christ. If we claim to be Christians, then we need to stand on Christ's word. When God leads us as Christians to take a step of Faith, He makes provisions. He is our sufficiency. God is our Source and Provider. Knowing His promises will make our Faith firm. When our Faith is challenged, we should stand firm because God will never forsake us (Deuteronomy 31 vs 6; Hebrews 13 vs 5–6). Believers must look to Jesus the author and finisher of our Faith. When God leads, we have to follow, because He always has a plan for us. We need to have Faith in Him. Personally, I travelled many miles to Zimbabwe to discover that land mines were planted everywhere due to the struggle for independence.

Never Underestimate The Background Work Of God

We drove everywhere in Zimbabwe to preach, yet no land mine exploded on or around us. This was a great miracle that God did in our lives. He said He will never forsake us and He proved it. We didn't see the work in progress, but we saw the final result, and this manifested by Him protecting us throughout. It is a fact that God always works in the background to make sure we, His children, are protected in every aspect of our lives. We just need to have total Faith in Him, and never underestimate His works.

Chapter Eight

FAITH CAN BE SHAKEN

There is no doubt that as Christians our Faith will be challenged. Sometimes Faith can be shaken, even when we consider the most Faith-based people. There are various cases like this. A typical example is Abraham, who was regarded as the father of Faith (Hebrews 11 vs 8-19; Romans 4 vs 9-13). Abraham didn't only love God, but he had Faith in Him, one that seemed unshakeable. However, when we look at what transpired in Genesis 17 vs. 15-21, we realise that when God spoke to Abraham about his wife, Sarah, going to be a mother, Abraham had doubts and reminded God about him being 100 years old and Sarah being 90 years old. Making it physically and humanly impossible for Sarah to have children. At this point, Abraham being a man of Faith, the one God promised men and nations would be blessed from (Genesis 12 vs 2), couldn't understand God's assertion about him. His Faith was challenged against time, against his age and that of his wife, and against their physical ability. Abraham couldn't comprehend how the youth of his wife could be renewed, and this clearly created doubts in his mind as a human. But God's ways are not our ways. (Isaiah 55 vs. 8-9). God indeed made what seemed impossible in Abraham and Sarah's eyes possible, and Sarah indeed gave birth to a son called Isaac (Genesis 21 vs 1-7).

One thing we need to realise is that no one is above challenges when it comes to exercising Faith. Having our Faith challenged has nothing to do with the number of times or years we have been exercising Faith. If someone like Abraham could have his Faith challenged and even shaken, then we need to know we can't get to a level where we feel complacent; a place where we feel too confident that we regard ourselves unchallengeable and unshakable when it comes to Faith. Even people who have seen first-hand, the work of Jesus Christ our personal Lord and Saviour, have had their Faith shaken. A typical example is Thomas. One whose name is almost synonymous to doubts; 'doubting Thomas'.

Thomas was a disciple of Jesus Christ. He followed him around, listened to His words, and I believe he saw Him prove Himself several times, through miracles and making the seemingly impossible, possible. But when Jesus Christ rose from the dead and appeared to some of the disciples' while Thomas was away, it created an avenue for Thomas' Faith to be tested. When the disciples who had seen Jesus Christ after He rose from the dead told Thomas about it, he doubted, he didn't believe that the person whom he had seen perform miracles and make all the impossible things come to pass could rise from the dead. To Thomas, the person he called Saviour and believed was the son of God couldn't have risen from the dead; he wanted proof so he asked if he could put his fingers in the wound from the nailed palms of Christ (John 20 vs 24-29). Thomas didn't believe Jesus had risen from the dead until He had proof. This event in the bible teaches a lot of lessons.

Faith Can Be Shaken

Even if we work with the Master, we are prone to doubts and our Faith can be challenged. Thomas wasn't the only one that worked closely with Christ who had his Faith shaken.

Peter also had his Faith challenged when he was with Christ. Peter was in the boat while Jesus was standing on the water, and Jesus asked him to come to Him. Peter stood on Jesus' word and took the steps. At that moment, he had Faith in His word. He however had his faith tested while he was walking towards Jesus. His Faith was challenged by the fact that he was walking on water. He looked down and saw that he was really walking on water and I believe the human instinct kicked in and reminded him that it was impossible to do so. With the setting-in of doubt, he started to sink. But one interesting thing happened, Peter knew he had lost Faith. At that point, he didn't focus on struggling to stay afloat alone. In the midst of his struggle, he called on the one person he knew could save him. He called on Jesus for help, and he was saved (Matthew 14 vs 24-31). We could say Peter failed when his

The Step of Faith

Faith was being tested, but of course Jesus Christ didn't fail him in this case. He was there to save him.

We need to be aware that our Faith will always be challenged, in most cases, it will be shaken. This is an important fact that we can't ignore. But the most important thing is what we do when our Faith is challenged. We need to know that the Lord is always with us, the only One who can calm waters in the midst of storms (Mark 4 vs 35-41).

From the bible, we know for a fact that Jesus isn't moved by circumstances that put us on edge or make us panic. In Matthew 8 vs 23-27 there was a heavy storm at sea, causing His disciples to panic, but Jesus was fast asleep. When we put ourselves in the exact situation the disciples found themselves, we would appreciate their fears. Personally, I can't imagine myself in the middle of the sea, with no land in sight, no rescue boat around, but with just people panicking around me, coupled with a storm that could destroy the boat in which I find myself in seconds. It is even more difficult for me to visualize the turbulence, the unsettling feeling of not knowing when you would be thrown in the sea, the inability to take proper steps as a result of the instabilities in the boat. This circumstance is enough to make anyone panic, at least those who don't have a death wish. I know I would be scared. But in the midst of all this, Jesus was sleeping peacefully. Sometimes I try to imagine how the chaos didn't wake him up, but I remind myself that if you are the Master of all, you can't be shaken by your creation, and Jesus proved this by calming the sea. When His disciples woke Him up out of fear, He spoke to the storm and it listened.

One would wonder why Jesus' disciples were even scared in the first place. They have been with Him for a long time, and have seen Him do wonders, miracles that were beyond their imagination; life-changing experiences that they have professed to others, yet they were scared. The question is, why would you be walking with the Master and be afraid? Why would you know the Lord is with you and be afraid? The simple answer to this is that we as humans are prone to doubt, and this exposes us to situations where our Faith can be challenged. But just as the disciples did, that is when we need to call on God. The whole essence of having Christ is to save us, whether it is when we are in trouble or when we need our Faith reinforced.

Many have seen signs and wonders and have worked with the Master, and have seen the supernatural, but they have definitely been challenged when it comes to their Faith. When we look at the references from the bible, from Abraham to the disciples of Christ, we will realise that even in the presence of doubt, God remained sovereign, and did what He wanted to do regardless of their doubts. Sometimes we become Faithless, but God remains faithful (2 Timothy 2 vs 13).

I used the examples in the bible to highlight the point that our Faith will come under attack, or be challenged. These are events that we can all read for ourselves and verify. There are many stories that I have been linked with in this regard. I remember many years ago, one of my member's daughter wanted to travel from Ghana to the US, to join her husband. She tried several times to secure a visa, but to no avail could not succeed. They were hoping for a reunion, but it just wasn't happening. Her husband even bought a car for her in the US and parked it in the garage, awaiting her arrival. He also had other plans for her to make life better and she was looking forward to enjoying the American dream. But all of these dreams were contingent upon her securing a visa, which seemed unattainable at the time. She prayed and fasted but nothing was happening. When she came to see me, it was clear she had lost hope, but I encouraged her to maintain her Faith. I asked her to envision herself driving the car her husband had bought for her in the US, and to see herself in the kitchen the husband had built for her. I told her to believe that Jesus would make that dream come true. We prayed and we continuously called on God. The seemingly impossible dream came to reality. She was finally granted the visa, and was able to join with her husband. She ended up being a nurse in the US, and became a permanent resident there. At one point this reality was bleak, it was impossible, so she lost Faith, but God made it happen.

There are times when even people close to us make it difficult to exercise our Faith. This is a reality we need to come to terms with. I know a couple who had been married for over 12 years and were struggling to have children. They did everything physically possible to have children, but nothing came out of it. At a point the mother of the woman asked her daughter to divorce the husband, because the daughter was her only child and she wanted grandchildren. Being a wealthy woman, she threatened her daughter that if she didn't divorce her husband, she was going to remove her from her will. This was more like disowning her child. Regardless of this pressure, her daughter refused to divorce her husband. All through these rough times, they were praying and hoping on God, but nothing was happening. Their Faith was clearly challenged. At one point, they gave up and accepted that they were never going to have children.

One day the couple came to church and I was preaching on expectancy. At that point I didn't know them, but before I concluded my preaching I made this statement *"you're here this morning, you're believing that your husband will give you a child, your husband can't give you a child he's not God; husbands you're believing that your wife will give you a child, she isn't God she can't give you a child; it is only God that gives us children, so expect your child from God!"* When they heard this statement, they realised that they had made a big mistake by expecting children from each other and not from God. They were praying for years, but they were laying more emphasis on their own ability to have children. Just a month after they heard my message and realised their mistake, the woman conceived and gave birth to a son. Our Faith will be challenged and shaken in most instances. Some of us will even give up entirely, but God who is sovereign is always able to come through.

The Step of Faith

My Faith in God has been tested several times even after many years in my ministry. When this happens, I usually remind myself that once God has directed me and I take that step of Faith, He will surely make provisions for me, no matter how unlikely it is. In my ministry, many times I have been homeless, and this tested my Faith. However, I still find my way back to having a steadfast Faith in God, and He has never failed me. Faith needs good shock absorbers and from my experience, it lies in the word of God.

Chapter Nine

CONCLUSION

Faith is a phenomenon that is complex to evaluate, however we know from universal definitions that Faith is defined as a strong belief in, or trust in someone or something, or a belief in a god or gods. This definition doesn't make the evaluation of Faith easy; it certainly also doesn't make the measurement of Faith easy. All of these are as a result of Faith being a mental process. This makes evaluating people's actions the closest tool available for us to rely on when accessing Faith or the level of Faith one possesses. However, since actions in most cases are based on circumstances, it becomes apparent that we can't fully understand people's actions unless we are faced with the same circumstance, they find themselves in. This implies that we can't fully understand people's levels of Faith or the associated actions with regards to their Faith, unless we are in the same circumstance they find themselves. This points to the logical conclusion that we need to be considerate when we access people's actions with regards to their level of Faith.

Regardless of the complexity of Faith, and the different meanings or dimensions people attach to it, the Christian Faith has a more narrowed and specific definition. Faith in Christianity isn't a total belief in gods or things, but a total belief in God. With Christian Faith, there are no 'ORs, it is the total surrender to the Supreme God, Jesus Christ. Without the total surrender to Him, we can't call ourselves Christians. This implies that if we don't have Faith in Christ, then we can't call ourselves Christians. In essence, Faith in itself is the ground on which Christianity is built, and the Bible is covered with proof of this (Hebrews 11:6; Mark 11 vs 22-24) some of which has been highlighted throughout this book.

Scriptures have shown that if we have Faith in Christ, He is sure to answer all our prayers and direct our path (Matthew 21 vs 22). We need to bear in mind that, believing in

Conclusion

Christ makes us Christians and it is key for our salvation, but it doesn't immune us from observing rules or principles in Christianity. What this means is that there are actions that we take or we wish to take as Christians that requires the observations of certain rules, one of such action is taking a step of Faith.

Being a Christian doesn't immune us from observing the required principles when we want to take a step of Faith. This is a rule I ignored as a young believer. I was clueless as to what I needed to do before taking any step of Faith, and this almost cost me my life. But God being merciful spared me, and in essence, saved me from my ignorance. I am grateful to God for not only saving me, but also teaching me important lessons in life.

From my experience, I can say with a high level of certainty that to be successful in any step of Faith we need to acknowledge the precursors to taking steps of Faith. These precursors are; hearing the Word of God, Praying, and Fasting.

The Step of Faith

These are spiritual exercises that can't be ignored as they are important for directing our steps, clearing our paths, and strengthening us while we embark on a step of Faith. These are exercises I have engaged in several times as a minister of God, and they have never failed me. But we also have to bear in mind that while we consider the spiritual, we can't ignore the physical.

The physical environment can't be ignored when taking a step of Faith. This includes where we find ourselves, and in some instances our physical state. There have been indications that to some extent it is easier to take steps of Faith when we are in systems or in an environment that seems to be conducive or productive as compared to those that are not. A chaotic system can give an indication that the status quo can't be changed, giving room to our human tendency to give up and not have Faith. It is based on this that we need to be considerate when we talk to people about their level of Faith, or when we try to evaluate their actions with regards to Faith.

Conclusion

For example, we shouldn't expect someone living in a war-torn area such as Syria to exhibit the same level of enthusiasm when we talk about Faith, as someone from a relatively stable country like the US would.

Our physical environment should also make us mindful of our step of Faith with regards to how it affects those around us. We can't be selfish and ignore how our actions affect others. The fact that we are taking a step of Faith in the name of God doesn't mean we shouldn't be considerate about the people around us. I remember when I was young, I had the fire in me to constantly move by Faith. This wasn't necessarily a bad thing, but there were a lot of things I ignored, and years later I realised that I should have been more considerate. A typical example is how I sometimes left my wife and children alone, ignoring how they felt while I took my step of Faith. Now, I would definitely do things differently. This writing creates an avenue for others to learn from my mistakes.

The Step of Faith

There were also steps I took years ago, that I can't take now, because the world has changed so much. There is so much evil in the world now. We constantly need to think of the risk levels when we are taking steps of Faith, and also the risks we expose others to. In essence, when we are taking steps of Faith, we need to be logical.

There is no doubt that our environment plays a key part in *if and how* we take the step of Faith. However, we know from the bible that whatever situation we find ourselves in, God always makes a way. On the back of this, we should also note that even in systems that work, there is the tendency for us to become complacent, and disregard God's ability. Hence, making us feel there is no need to have Faith in God, since things usually work for us anyway. This is however the wrong direction to take. We can't disregard God even in situations where things are going smoothly, because He gives us the so-called things we are enjoying. Regardless of where we find ourselves, or our physical condition, we need to discipline ourselves in order to not lose sight of God, and meditating on His word constantly is a sure way to achieve this.

One of the most important things to do as people of Faith is to constantly fix our eyes on God. This is because there are a lot of challenges associated with Faith, and our Faith can be shaken. From my experience I know that when taking a step of Faith, we are exposed to various challenges from different avenues. These challenges don't only have the tendency to frustrate us, but they also hold the potential of making us lose our Faith. Regardless of our age or the number of years we have lived as Christians, we shouldn't feel that we have reached a level in Christianity where we become immune to the challenges associated with Faith. Even those who were with Christ had their Faith challenged and shaken, like Peter and Thomas. For us to beat this, we need to always be ready for these challenges and rely totally on God to see us through. Asking God for wisdom is also key, because we don't only battle with spiritual challenges but also physical challenges, which requires wisdom in most cases to deal with. As the Bible points out, wisdom is key (Proverbs 4 vs 6, 8 vs 11).

While we do our part physically and rely on God to do His part, we should always bear in mind that He is always working in the background. We might not see it, but we need to know that whatever happens He is working behind and making things happen for our own good. This implies that even when things seem to be bad or not going as planned, we should know that there is a reason for that. Of course, as humans, our tendency to worry and complain is bound to set in, but from my experience, even the worse situations have turned out to be advantageous for me. The bible says all things work together for our good (Romans 8 vs. 28), and we need to always remember this.

Notes

Notes

TOPIC: _____

Notes

Notes

TOPIC: _____

www.ingramcontent.com/pod-product-compliance
Lightning Source LLC
Chambersburg PA
CBHW051656040426
42446CB00009B/1163